The Life of Guy Fawkes

Emma Lynch

Heinemann LIBRARY

H www.heinemann.co.uk/library

Visit our website to find out more information about **Heinemann Library** books.

To order:

☎ Phone 44 (0) 1865 888066

🖹 Send a fax to 44 (0) 1865 314091

🖥 Visit the Heinemann Bookshop at www.heinemann.co.uk/library to browse our catalogue and order online.

First published in Great Britain by Heinemann Library, Halley Court, Jordan Hill, Oxford OX2 8EJ, part of Harcourt Education.
Heinemann is a registered trademark of Harcourt Education Ltd.

Editorial: Lucy Thunder and Harriet Milles
Design: Richard Parker and
    Tinstar Design Ltd (www.tinstar.co.uk)
Illustrations: Tim Beard and Gerry Ball
    (Eikon Illustrations)
Picture Research: Melissa Allison and Fiona Orbell
Production: Camilla Smith

Originated by Repro Multi-Warna
Printed and bound in China by
    South China Printing Company

ISBN 0 431 18102 0 (hardback)
09 08 07 06 05
10 9 8 7 6 5 4 3 2 1

ISBN 0 431 18167 5 (paperback)
10 09 08 07 06
10 9 8 7 6 5 4 3 2 1

British Library Cataloguing in Publication Data
Emma Lynch
Guy Fawkes. – (The Life of)
941'.061'092
A full catalogue record for this book is available from the British Library.

Acknowledgements
The Publishers would like to thank the following for permission to reproduce photographs:
pp. 4, 16 Bridgeman Art Library/Private Collection; pp. 5, 25 TopFoto/Arena Images; pp. 7, 10, 14, 15 Mary Evans Picture Library; p. 6 Dean & Chapter of York; p. 8 E & E Picture Library; p. 9 Bettmann/Corbis; p. 11 Bridgeman Art Library/Prado, Madrid, Spain; p. 12 Bridgeman Art Library/Galleria degli Uffizi, Florence, Italy; p. 18 Ashmolean Museum; p. 19 Museum of London; p. 21 Topham Picturepoint; p. 20 Martin Jones/Corbis; p. 22 Bridgeman Art Library/Harrogate Museum & Art Gallery; p. 26 Getty Images/Hulton Archive; p. 27 Historic Royal Palaces

Cover photograph of Guy Fawkes, reproduced with permission of Mary Evans Picture Library.
Page icons: Hemera PhotoObjects.

Every effort has been made to contact copyright holders of any material reproduced in this book. Any omissions will be rectified in subsequent printings if notice is given to the Publishers.

Contents

Words shown in the text in bold, **like this**, are explained in the Glossary.

Who was Guy Fawkes?

Guy Fawkes is famous because he tried to kill King James I. About 400 years ago, he took part in a plan to blow up the **Houses of Parliament**.

This picture shows the Houses of Parliament today. They are in Westminster, London.

Every year, we remember the Gunpowder Plot on Bonfire Night.

The plan was called the **Gunpowder Plot**. It was to take place on 5 November 1605. Guy was caught before he could carry out the plan.

Early years

Guy Fawkes was born on 13 April 1570. His mother and father were **Protestants**. Guy's father died when Guy was only eight years old.

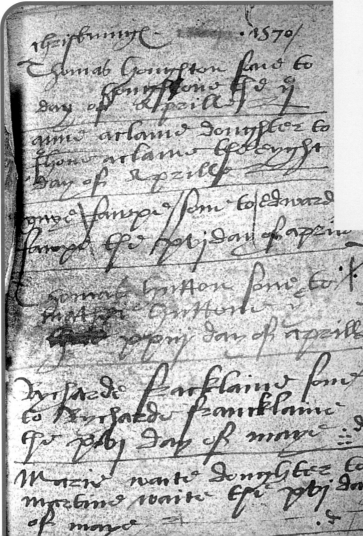

Guy's **christening**, was on 16 April 1570. It was written down in the church of Saint Michael-le-Belfrey, York.

Guy Fawkes was born and grew up in Stonegate in York.

Guy's mother got married again to a **Catholic** man. Elizabeth I was queen at that time. She was a Protestant. She wanted everyone else to be Protestants too.

Becoming a Catholic

At that time, people were told they had to go to **Protestant** churches. Many people still wanted to be **Catholics**. They had to pray in secret.

Some people hid Catholic **priests** in secret places in their houses, to keep them safe. These were called 'priest holes'.

Guy became a Catholic while he was at school. His friends at school were John and Christopher Wright. They were Catholics too. Later, they also took part in the **Gunpowder Plot**.

This picture shows Christopher and John Wright when they were older. Another Catholic, Thomas Percy, is with them.

Fighting for Spain

When he was about 23, Guy left England. He became a soldier in the Spanish army. Spain was a **Catholic** country. Guy wanted to fight for the Catholic Church.

The Spanish fought fierce sea battles against the Dutch and the French.

This is King Philip II of Spain.

Guy changed his name to 'Guido'. It means Guy in Spanish. He was well liked by the Spanish soldiers. Guy asked the Spanish king to help Catholics in England.

Getting it wrong

In 1603, Queen Elizabeth I died and James I became king. James was a Protestant. Guy thought that all **Catholics** in England would want to get rid of the new king. He was wrong!

James I was crowned king on 25 July 1603.

Most English Catholics did not want any more trouble. Guy had been away for too long. He did not understand what was happening in England.

King James I was welcomed by Catholics and **Protestants.**

The Gunpowder Plot

Guy moved back to London in May 1604. He joined a small group of English **Catholics**. They **plotted** to kill King James I and take over **Parliament**.

This picture shows eight of the thirteen plotters.

The plan was to blow up Parliament on 5 November 1605. King James would be there on that day. The King and many other important people would be killed.

Thomas Percy

Guido Fawkes

Robert Catesby

Thomas Winter

The plotters were angry because King James I had made life even harder for Catholics.

Planning and plotting

In Spring 1605, one of the **plotters** paid for a **cellar** under the **Houses of Parliament**.

These cellars are where the plot would be carried out.

Guy had learnt about gunpowder in the army.

The plotters stored **36** barrels of **gunpowder** in the cellar. They covered them with iron bars and firewood. Guy was asked to blow them up.

The plot is found out

On 26 October 1605, a **Catholic** called Lord Mounteagle was sent a letter. The letter told him not to go to the opening of **Parliament** on 5 November.

The letter made Lord Mounteagle think that something bad was going to happen.

> my lord out of the loue i beare
> i haue a caer of youer preseruacion therfor i woulde...
> aduyse yowe as yowe tender youer lyf to deuys some
> epscuse to shift of youer attendance at this parleament
> for god and man hathe concurred to punishe the wickednes
> of this tyme and thinke not slightlye of this aduertisment
> but retyere youre self into youre countri wheare yowe
> maye expect the euent in safti for thowghe theare be no
> apparance of anai stir yet i saye they shall receyue a terrible
> blowe this parleament and yet they shall not seie who
> hurts them this councel is not to be contemned because
> it maye do yowe good and can do yowe no harme for the
> dangere is passed as soon as yowe haue burnt the letter
> and i hope god will gine yowe the grace to mak good
> use of it to whose holy proteccion i comend yowe
>
> To the ryght honorable
> The lord mounteagle

18

Guy had **fuses** in his pockets to light the gunpowder.

On 4 November, soldiers went to search Parliament. They went into the **cellars** and found barrels of **gunpowder**. They also found Guy Fawkes.

To the Tower

Guy was taken to the Tower of London. On 8 November he **signed** a **confession**. He would not name the other **plotters**. James I said that Guy should be **tortured**.

This is the Tower of London where Guy was taken.

On 9 November Guy signed another confession. This time, he named all the other plotters. His name on the second confession is very wobbly. This is probably because he had been tortured.

Look at the difference between Guy's writing on the two confessions.

Death for treason

The other **plotters** were caught and tried for **treason**. On 31 January 1606, Guy and three other plotters were put to death in Westminster.

King James I wanted to meet the man who had tried to kill him.

Guy was very weak after being **tortured**.

The plotters were hanged and dragged through the streets. Then they were cut into quarters. Their heads were stuck on poles, as a warning to other people.

Why is Guy famous?

We remember Guy because he tried to kill the king. The **Gunpowder Plot** did nothing to help **Catholics** at that time. It made life even harder for them.

'Remember, remember
The fifth of November,
*Gunpowder, **treason** and plot.*
I see no reason
Why gunpowder treason
Should ever be forgot.'

This poem was written soon after the Gunpowder Plot.

The 'guy' that we put on our bonfires is supposed to be Guy Fawkes.

Today, we remember Guy Fawkes on 5 November every year. We celebrate Bonfire Night because the plot did not work.

More about Guy

There are books and websites about Guy Fawkes and the **Gunpowder Plot**. We can see objects from that time in **museums**.

This lantern is in a museum in Oxford. It may have been Guy's.

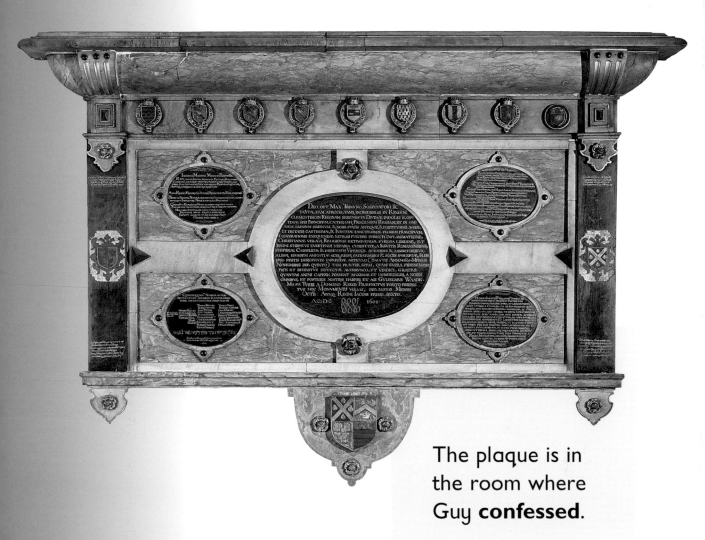

The plaque is in the room where Guy **confessed**.

We can visit the **Houses of Parliament** and the Tower of London. There is a **plaque** in the Tower of London. It tells the story of the Gunpowder Plot.

Fact file

- There are only a few pictures of Guy Fawkes. They were painted after his death. We do not know if the artists ever saw him!

- During the **Gunpowder Plot**, Guy Fawkes did not use his real name. He called himself John Johnson instead.

- There were 13 Gunpowder Plotters. They were Robert Catesby, Christopher and John Wright, Thomas Percy, Thomas and Robert Wintour, Guy Fawkes, Robert Keyes, Thomas Bates, John Grant, Ambrose Rookwood, Francis Tresham and Sir Everard Digby.

Timeline

1570	Guy Fawkes is born in York on 13 April
1578	Guy's father, Edward Fawkes, dies
about 1588	Guy's mother remarries
1593/4	Guy leaves England to fight for the Spanish army
1603	Guy travels to Spain to ask King Philip II to help English **Catholics**
1604	Guy returns to London and meets the other members of the Gunpowder Plot
1605	The Gunpowder Plot is discovered on 4 November
1606	Guy is put to death in London on 31 January

Glossary

Catholic member of the Church of Rome, led by the Pope

cellar room under a house or other building

christening becoming a member of the Christian Church

confession when someone admits they have done something

fuses cords that can be lit to start a fire

gunpowder mixture of chemicals that explodes when lit

Houses of Parliament building where the government meets to decide how to run the country

museum place where important pieces of art or parts of history are kept for people to see

plaque special sign to remember something

plot a secret plan

priest someone who performs Catholic religious acts

Protestant member of the Church of England

sign write your name on something to show you agree with it

torture to hurt someone badly until they give you information

treason crime against the King or Queen and country

Find out more

Books

Famous People, Famous Lives: Guy Fawkes,
Harriet Castor (Franklin Watts, 2001)

How do we know about…?: The Gunpowder Plot,
Deborah Fox (Heinemann Library, 2002)

Stories from History: Gunpowder Guy,
Stewart Ross (Hodder Wayland, 2001)

Websites

www.guy-fawkes.com
Educational site about the history behind
Bonfire Night.

www.gunpowder-plot.org
Website of the Gunpowder Plot Society.

Places to Visit

The street where Guy was born at
Stonegate, York

Tower of London

Houses of Parliament, London

Index